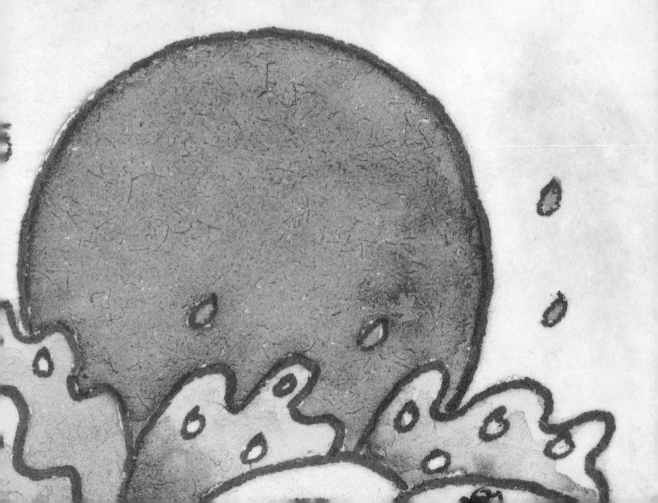

To David and Lotta

DAVID'S ARK

with love and thanks

This edition is
published and distributed
exclusively by
DISCOVERY TOYS
Pleasant Hill, CA

First published
in 1988 by
Walker Books, Ltd.
London

Printed in Italy

First American Edition

ISBN 0-939979-19-5

THE AMAZING STORY OF NOAH'S ARK

Written and illustrated by
Marcia Williams

DISCOVERY TOYS

Many, many summers

and winters ago,

God became angry with the world

because people had become so cruel.

They were stealing and lying,

cheating and fighting,

so God decided to destroy them all.

Everyone except for Noah and his family.

For Noah was a good, kind man.

"Noah," said God, "I will save all your family

and a male and female of every animal.

The rest will drown in a fearful flood."

Noah and his family worked hard building the ark.

They chopped down trees

and sawed the logs.

They hammered the wood

and covered it with pitch.

Other people pointed their fingers

and laughed at Noah.

They thought he was silly

talking of floods and building an ark.

Noah worked on and on

until the ark was completed.

Then God told him to start loading up,

for in seven days the great rains would start.

Noah thought he might have trouble

catching all the animals. But he didn't,

for God had told them to go to Noah

and climb aboard his ark.

The animals went in two by two –

giraffes and birds and elephants,

bears and sheep and spotted lizards,

lions and seals, zebras and snakes,

walruses, guinea fowl and pigs, and

WELC

ARD !

rhinos and camels and ladybugs,

leopards and rabbits and horses,

a cow and bull and a pair of goats,

all the tiny insects which Noah could hardly see.

It was hard work squeezing them all in!

But when the first drops of rain fell,

the last insect found a bed

SLAM!

and the great doors were slammed shut.

For forty days and forty nights the rain fell.

The ark was lifted above the earth.

The waters rose higher and higher

until even the tallest mountain was covered.

Not a creature on earth was left alive.

And still it rained on and on.

For many days the ark drifted.

Then God sent a wind over the earth, and

the waters went.

Finally, after seven long months, the ark came to rest on Mount Ararat. Noah opened the window and let out a raven. But it could find nowhere to land.

Noah opened
the window again

and sent out a dove.

It flew far and wide

but could find nowhere
to rest.

Seven days later

Noah sent out the
dove once more.

In the evening it returned
to the ark.

In its beak it carried
an olive branch.

This told Noah that soon
the waters would dry.

ONE	TWO	THREE	FOUR	FIVE	SIX	SEVEN

He waited another seven days

and then sent out the dove again.

This time it did not return to the ark.

HOORAY!

Noah opened the window and saw that the earth was dry.

He pushed open the great door.

Out rushed Noah's family and all the animals,

joyful to walk on land again.

Noah built an altar to thank God.

God was so pleased that He promised Noah

never to flood the world again.

A rainbow appeared as a sign of His promise.

Noah was very happy to see this.

He made a new home and planted a vineyard

and lived to a very great age

with his family and all the creatures of the ark

and their many children.

So now, whenever it rains and you see a rainbow,

you can remember the story of Noah.